A CASE FOR
Calling

Also by ™Life@Work Co.™

A Case for Character
A Case for Skill
A Case for Serving

THE Life@Work Co.™

A CASE FOR
Calling

Discovering the Difference a Godly Man Makes in His Life at Work

DR. THOMAS ADDINGTON & DR. STEPHEN GRAVES

Cornerstone *Alliance*

FAYETTEVILLE, ARKANSAS 72702

Published by Cornerstone Alliance
Post Office Box 1928
Fayetteville, AR 72702

ISBN 1-890581-01-1

Cover design by Sean Womack of Cornerstone Alliance.

Printed in the United States of America

1 3 5 7 9 10 8 6 4 2

To our parents

Gordon and Bonnie Addington
and Evelyn Graves

You have always encouraged us
to live out our calling
Thank you
for that immeasurable gift.

Series Introduction

Our offices are on the fourth floor of the second tallest building in northwest Arkansas. We have an extraordinary view of the rolling hills of Fayetteville from our panoramic picture windows. Although our city is growing, it still has the feel of a small town. Almost everyone knows almost everyone.

From that vantage point we enjoy watching cycles of life unfold around us. Unlike some parts of the country, we benefit from the whole assortment of seasons. The snowy mantle of winter melts into the sweaty heat of summer, with all variations in between.

We also watch the daily routine of hundreds of businesses. At the start of a day we can see the lights of other businesses coming on, like eyes popping open after a good night's sleep. At the end of a day we witness those same lights going out. The next morning it begins all over again. Then again. Then again.

We talk to many men for whom that description sums up their work experience. People come and go, accounts open and close. Creditors get paid; customers get billed. We pick up; we deliver. We punch in; we punch out. The workday begins, then ends. We earn our money; we spend our money. The cycle is unrelenting and unending. Then the cycle quits, and we die.

Is that all there is? Is routine drudgery what a man should expect from his work life and career?

What is the difference in the behavior and experience of a Christian man in his work compared to that of a non-Christian man?

What does it mean to be a Christian who practices dentistry? Does it mean that I have Bible verses on my business card? Do I share Christ with patients while they are under anesthesia? Or perhaps I ought to treat only Christian patients. If someone doesn't pay me, should I send their bill into collections, or should I forgive the debt and maybe pay for it myself? Should I work longer hours to display an incredible work ethic? Or maybe I need to work shorter hours so that I can spend more time with my family or serve on a church or community committee. Do I pay my employees more than the national average? Or do I pay them less so they can learn to live by faith?

What does it mean to be a Christian plumber? Do I cut my rates for Christian customers? Should I work on Sunday, or do I fail to respond to a crisis that comes on the Sabbath? Perhaps I need to hand out gospel tracts to other subcontractors on the job. Should I release one of my crew if he's incompetent? Or are Christians bound to keep every employee on the payroll for life? What does the Bible say about work?

A number of years ago we came across a verse in the New Testament book of Acts that serves as God's final epitaph for King David:

> When David had served God's purpose in his own generation, he fell asleep. (Acts 13:36)

Those words complete a description of David found way back in the Old Testament book of Psalms:

> He chose David his servant and took him from the sheep pens; from tending the sheep he brought him to be the shepherd of his people Jacob, of Israel his inheritance. And David shepherded them with integrity of heart; with skillful hands he led them. (Psalm 78:70-72)

David was a shepherd, a musician, a soldier, and a king. He had a very busy, full, and successful career. We would like to use those verses about David as the basis for exploring the making of a godly man in and through his work world. This short series will consist of four parts:

....David...*served God's purpose...*:   A Case for Calling
He chose *David his servant...*:   A Case for Serving
....David shepherded them
with *integrity of heart.*   A Case for Character
....with *skillful hands* he led them: A Case for Skill

So, we are back to one of our questions from above. Is work basically an unending and unfulfilling cycle of activity? Answer: it depends. On what? On whether or not I know God.

According to King Solomon, one of the wisest and wealthiest men of all time:

A man can do nothing better than to eat and drink and find satisfaction in his work. This too, I see, is from the hand of God.... *To the man who pleases him, God gives wisdom, knowledge and happiness, but to the sinner he gives the task of gathering and storing up wealth to hand it over to the one who pleases God.* (Ecclesiastes 2:24-26; italics added)

Without God in my life, I might be driven, full of ambition, and very successful. I might even make it to the pinnacle of my profession. But I will not enjoy my work over time. It will not bring me fulfillment. I will be on a treadmill.

These books address a Christian man in the workplace. The definition and clarity that the Bible brings to a man and his work world are reserved for those who enjoy a personal relationship with Jesus. If you don't know Him, we strongly urge you to invite Him into your life. Then join us in exploring the topic of work in the incredibly rich, amazingly untapped pages of Scripture.

May the favor of the Lord our God rest upon us;
establish the work of our hands for us—
yes, establish the work of our hands. (Psalm 90:17)

A word about our writing style. As coauthors, we speak in the first person when telling a story that relates to one of us as individuals. But we do not identify who belongs to which story. To help unravel that mystery, the following are some personal characteristics that will help sort us out.

Steve is an avid fisherman who baited hooks as a young boy on the Mississippi Gulf Coast. His appetite for learning and his energy for making friends have trademarked his twenty-three years of ministry and business.

Tom grew up in Hong Kong as the son of a medical missionary. He spent a number of years driving eighteen-wheelers, and he has taught at three universities.

We live in Fayetteville, Arkansas, love Scripture, and work together as business partners. Our companies and colleagues do work in organizational consulting and publishing. We have a passion to understand biblical principles that apply to work.

Book Introduction

Calling happens.

All Christian men are called. Individually. In regards to their work. I have been created by God to do something God wants me to do. When I know my calling and live it out, I am actually and literally part of fulfilling God's purpose.

To realize that is unbelievably wonderful. What could possibly be more fulfilling? My question is not, "Am I called?" Instead, my quest through life is, "What is my calling?"

This book helps define what calling is, and helps identify how I know my calling. What we learn might surprise us. But then, God is pretty good at doing that.

He has called me.

Definition of Calling

God's personal invitation for me
to work on his agenda,
using the talents I've been given
in ways that are eternally significant.

"When David had served God's purpose in his own generation, he fell asleep" (Acts 13:36).

CONTENTS

CHAPTER ONE

What Calling Is

I love to fish. Every year I go on a fishing expedition with three of my friends. I always look forward to it. I always come back the better for it. I love to fish.

Three of those annual trips have been on the Buffalo River in the Ozark National Forest, right here in Arkansas. The last twenty-five miles of the Buffalo, just before it dumps into the White River, is a remote wilderness area with no road access. The water is pristine clear; the cliffs are awesome and incredible; there is wildlife of every kind everywhere. It is peaceful and serene; you almost never see any other people.

It takes us four days of floating and camping to fish all the way to the White River. You haven't really lived until you have done a little top-water smallmouth-bass fishing on the last twenty-five miles of the Buffalo.

But I will never forget the beginning of the first day the first time we went. As usual, we were equipment heavy. We loaded all our food, camping apparatus, and fishing gear into the flat-bottomed eighteen-foot riverboats. We waved good-bye to the toothless stranger who had promised to deliver our cars to us at the end of the trip. We shoved off. We were on our way.

Less than four hundred yards into the twenty-five-mile trip is a sharp bend to the right. As we approached the turn we heard a noise that sounded distinctly like a waterfall. Or perhaps, waterfalls. Then our eyes confirmed what our ears had heard. Directly ahead of us was a steep drop. I couldn't believe it. We had been in the water less than five minutes, our cars were gone, and no one even expected to see us for four days.

We were not happy. There was some grumbling and murmuring in the ranks along the line of: "I thought this was supposed to be the Buffalo, not Niagara." Then we huddled up and did all we knew to do. We got in the water and wrestled the boats, one by one, around the drop-off and through the rapids. Getting to four wonderful days of fishing meant that we had to navigate some rough water at the very beginning of the trip.

In the same way, getting to a meaningful career means that I first have to understand my calling. It is the initial key to figuring out my life at work.

As long as I have doubts about my calling, I will wonder if I am doing what I am supposed to be doing. Conversations with my wife will begin with words like: "I don't know, there just is something missing at work" or "I keep wondering if I should look into some other job possibilities" or "I wonder what else there is out there that might fit me better" or "I can't wait to retire so that I can..." or "I wish I could be more content with my work situation." If I don't know my calling, my work life will lack satisfaction.

But even more important, if I don't live out my calling, I compromise my ability to contribute to God's larger purpose with my work life and career. When the apostle Paul says, "David...served God's purpose in his own generation" (Acts 13:36), it is clear that God had a well-defined purpose for David's life work. In Scripture, "purpose" and "calling" are linked.

What is calling? What does it mean to be called in my work life? The answers to those questions are hidden in three principles from Scripture:

1. As a godly man I am called to serve God's purpose.

2. I have a calling that is work-specific.

3. God has given me a unique gift mix for my work.

It's to serve God's purpose.

My dad is a called man. He lives as meaningful a life as anyone I know. Well into retirement, he works tirelessly on a project that he believes God wants him to finish. But this current undertaking is only the latest evidence of God's obvious call on his seventy-plus-year life.

As a young man who had just completed seminary, he and Mom were convinced that they belonged in missions. When the mission organization told him that they really needed doctors, he promptly enrolled in medical school.

He arrived in Hong Kong in 1960 as a young physician to open an outpatient clinic. But because of the unmanageable influx of refugees from China, the Hong Kong Medical Department urged him to build an inpatient hospital. Evangel Hospital was dedicated in 1965 and to this day provides excellent medical care regardless of a patient's ability to pay.

Dad completed a residency in general surgery when it became clear that a surgeon was needed at the hospital, and none was available.

Later in his career when he returned to the United States, he practiced as a surgeon with the same sense of calling. He was at various times chief of surgery and chief of staff at a large hospital in St. Paul.

The list could go on. It would only emphasize and confirm what people who know my dad say about him: he is a man deeply aware of his calling.

Calling is God's personal invitation for me to work on *His* agenda, using the talents I've been given in ways that are eternally significant. To be called means I know that what I am doing is what God wants me to do. Furthermore, when I live within God's calling, not only does my work give me a sense of meaning, but it also fits into God's larger purpose.

Scripture clearly links my calling with God's purpose: "We know that in all things God works for the good of those who love him, who have been called according to his purpose" (Romans 8:28). My individual calling is absolutely connected with His purpose. I am being called in order to fit into His purpose.

My work is not some arbitrary and random choice that makes no difference. Its primary objective is not to put food on the table and provide a comfortable retirement. My individual, personal, just-me work calling is part of God's larger agenda in history. I actually have a part in God's plan.

The biblical concept of calling is confusing if we don't understand the difference and connection between calling, purpose, and meaning. They are not the same thing, but they are closely connected.

PURPOSE

Purpose in Scripture is synonymous with God's sovereign design, His overarching view of history, what He is accomplishing. Very few men in the Bible knew exactly what His purpose was during their lifetime. Some of the prophets did, at least to some extent. We know God's purpose only if He chooses to reveal it to us.

We are to serve God's purpose, whatever it is, even though we do not necessarily know all the details. Here is what we do know:

1. God operates off of a master plan, even though He doesn't always tell us what it is.

2. God specifically fits each of us as Christians into the larger workings of His overall plan.

3. We serve His purpose through faith by knowing His calling on our lives.

We meet men who think their purpose will be fulfilled whenever they make it to the next rung on the ladder or whenever they become their own boss and launch their own company. They are being pulled to do something bigger, but that search for purpose is always outside their grasp.

As Christian men, we know our work has purpose because we are serving a God whose purpose is bigger than us. To look up into the night sky at the end of the day and know that our work and life are part of His bigger plan supplies an inner joy and satisfaction that can come from nothing else.

CALLING

If purpose is something I have to serve, calling is something I need to know. Calling is what I do individually to fit into God's purpose. Some verses about calling refer to God's call on my life to become His child, as well as His call on my life regarding work or vocation. Other Scripture passages talk specifically about God's calling concerning work. Because I am "called according to His purpose," it is imperative that I discover exactly what my calling is. According to Ephesians: "In him we were also chosen [or called], having been predestined according to the plan of him who works out everything in conformity with the purpose of his will" (Ephesians 1:11).

God calls us to serve in a way that is consistent with how He has designed us. Finding my calling is about learning how God has designed me to serve Him.

MEANING

God's purpose is something I serve. My calling is something I know. Meaning is something I am to enjoy. If I am accurately living out my calling, I will experience the incredible sense of meaning from my work that only God can provide.

King Solomon was one of the wisest and wealthiest men of all time. He was a very successful king with an innate sense of how to do a financial deal. But his special gift from God was in the realm of wisdom. He had plenty of it.

Solomon wrote Ecclesiastes near the end of his life. He devotes portions of the Old Testament book to different topics, like wisdom, pleasure, and knowledge. But one entire part is devoted to work. In that section Solomon hammers at the theme that a godly man will find meaning, satisfaction, and fulfillment in his work:

A man can do nothing better than to eat and drink and find satisfaction in his work. This too, I see, is from the hand of God, for without him, who can eat or find enjoyment? (2:24-25)

I know that there is nothing better for men than to be happy and do good while they live. That every man may eat and drink, and find satisfaction in all his toil—this is the gift of God. (3:12-13)

So I saw that there is nothing better for a man than to enjoy his work, because that is his lot. (3:22)

Then I realized that it is good and proper for a man to eat and drink, and to find satisfaction in his toilsome labor under the sun during the few days of life God has given him—for this is his lot. (5:18)

Who receives the gift of work-related meaning? Everyone? Negative. Only those who are godly:

To the man who pleases him, God gives wisdom, knowledge and happiness, but to the sinner he gives the task of gathering and storing up wealth to hand it over to the one who pleases God. (2:26)

A non-Christian in the work world does not have nearly the sense of meaning in his career that a Christian experiences. He does the work. But he does not receive the same enjoyment, the same meaning, the same satisfaction available to a Christian. Only a Christian can serve God's purpose, can know God's calling, and can experience God's gift of meaning.

We are to serve purpose. We are to know calling. We are to enjoy meaning.

It's work-specific.

Jeremiah was one of God's prophets who played a crucial role in Old Testament Jewish history. The record of his calling gives us a unique window into what God has in mind for us regarding our work.

God set Jeremiah apart before he was even born, with a specific work purpose in mind: "Before you were born I set you apart," God said. Why? Because, "I appointed you as a prophet to the nations" (Jeremiah 1:5).

In this passage, Jeremiah's life had purpose because his work had purpose.

All men are called to work. Work is not a curse. Genesis documents God's work agenda for Adam before the Fall: "The Lord God took the man and put him in the Garden of Eden to work it and take care of it" (2:15).

In the next chapter we see God's work agenda after the Fall: "So the Lord God banished him from the Garden of Eden to work the ground from which he had been taken" (3:23).

Work is not a curse. But the curse—that came as a result of the Fall—made work much harder:

Cursed is the ground because of you; *through painful toil you will eat of it all the days of your life. It will produce thorns and thistles for you, and you will eat the plants of the field. By the sweat of your brow you will eat your food until you return to the ground,* since from it you were taken; for dust you are and to dust you will return. (Genesis 3:17-19; italics added)

The curse added a real sense of "sweat" and "making a living is going to be hard," but it did not remove the dignity and meaning from work. Nowhere in Scripture is work to be avoided. Nowhere in Scripture is work described as an unfortunate necessity that we must do only so that we can do "real fun stuff" like vacations, weekends, and retirements. Work is not a punishment or an afterthought. Quite the opposite, my calling from Jesus is work-specific. That all means that we should bring a tremendous energy and enthusiasm with us to work.

I drove tractor-trailer rigs for several years. It was always interesting to sit in the driver's lounge and listen to other drivers talk while our trucks were being loaded. Regardless of where I was in the country, the discussion revolved around the following four topics (the language has been sanitized):

1. My dispatcher is incompetent; he is out to get me and I am out to get him.

2. My job does not pay enough.

3. My company always tries to cheat me out of what they owe me.
4. No state trooper ever cuts me enough slack.

It took only five words to render everyone speechless, for a dead silence to descend on stunned men holding coffee cups. The words? "I like what I do." Whenever I uttered those words everyone sort of looked at the floor, cleared their throats, then announced that they needed to go check on when their trucks would be loaded. Conversation, as they knew it, was over.

If we are called, and if we are doing what we are called to do, we should be able to say that with conviction and without blushing. We ought to work hard and enjoy doing it. We should not have to apologize that we like to work and that we look forward to getting up in the morning and getting to the job. Nor should we have to buy into the notion that Mondays are terrible, compared with Fridays that are wonderful.

But we also need to be careful. Work is not the sum total of our life, nor was it ever meant to be. We must never hide behind our calling as an excuse for our work to own us in inappropriate ways. In our personal experience, and also from our conversations with hundreds of men over the years, there are at least three common traps that we need to run from:

1. Allowing work to drive me

There is a big difference between a driven man and a called man. Among other things, a driven man often allows the demands of the job to set the agenda for his life. "I am busy because I can't help it, because the job demands it," so the thinking goes. As work heats up, as the company grows, as the promotions come, as the number of customers increase, as the phone rings more often, I have no choice but to run faster, devote more hours, stay up later, get up earlier, travel more often.

As a called man, I will work very hard. But it is Jesus who is calling me, not my job. Unless we understand that distinction, the job that Jesus calls us to can actually end up calling us away from Jesus.

Drivenness emanates from internal restlessness, a never-satisfied striving, pride, and ego. Calling comes from knowing what I am supposed to do to fit into God's overarching purpose. It is Jesus who calls me, and in doing so He brings satisfaction, rest, a sense of togetherness, completeness, and whole-ness. The Jesus who calls us also calls out to us:

> Come to me, all you who are weary and burdened, and
> I will give you rest. Take my yoke upon you and learn
> from me, for I am gentle and humble in heart, and you
> will find rest for your souls. For my yoke is easy and
> my burden is light. (Matthew 11:28-30)

2. *Asking work to supply my identity*

When I became a Christian my name was recorded in the Lamb's Book of Life. Nowhere does Scripture indicate that my occupation will be recorded alongside my name. My identity comes from Christ.

How Paul saw himself, before he met Jesus, was directly tied to what he did as a Pharisee. His work supplied his iden-tity. One gets the impression that the list was well rehearsed:

> Circumcised on the eighth day, of the people of Israel,
> of the tribe of Benjamin, a Hebrew of Hebrews; in
> regard to the law, a Pharisee; as for zeal, persecuting the
> church; as for legalistic righteousness, faultless.
> (Philippians 3:5-6)

But after he became a Christian, he switched his identity from his work to his Lord: "But whatever was to my profit I now consider loss for the sake of Christ. I want to know Christ" (Philippians 3:7, 10).

3. *Using work to ignore my family*

A number of years ago I was with the founder of a major retailer as he addressed a group. In a moment of candor, the man related that members of his family were unhappy with all the time he was spending growing the company. He kept promising his wife, "Just one more store." Finally, his wife quit asking and he stopped promising, because both of them knew he was going to continue regardless.

We no longer have any excuse for not giving our families a balanced portion of our time and attention. Promise Keepers has addressed more men on that topic than any other topic. Authors like Gary Smalley, Wellington Boone, John Trent, James Dobson, Dennis Rainey, and Steve Farrar give us tremendous help in knowing how to be a good husband and father.

A calling to work does not take away from our privileges, obligations, joys, and pleasures of home life. If, over time, our work ends up stealing from the family, we have misunderstood how calling at work intersects with life at home.

It fits my unique gift mix

The men in our consulting company could not be more different in how we approach our work. We do similar tasks. We service the same clients. We share the same values. We use the same technology. But we could not be more different.

Some of us come at our work like engineers. Engineers operate best when a process is in place or can be designed. We love systems. We say things like " A good process turns out a good product." We are very organized. Our thinking is linear. We love to put information into specific categories. Knowing and following procedure are important. In our way of thinking, the best work is done behind the scenes, in preparation for rolling it out in public.

Others of us are in our best element as facilitators in a fast-moving meeting full of complex problems and difficult issues. We revel in free flow of information and ideas. Put us in a pressure situation where we have to think on our feet and figure things out on the spot, and we will shine. In our way of thinking, the best work is done in public. Behind-the-scenes preparation is OK, but it may not prove to be that relevant.

Then we have men who are a distinctive blend of a number of approaches. There is unbelievable richness in working with men with diverse makeup. We have different approaches to the same issues. Our perspectives are diverse and complement each other. The fact that we have different makeup is a good thing.

God gives us a unique gift mix for our work. We are all made differently. Listen to David reflect on the wonder of how God knows and uniquely makes up an individual:

O Lord, you have searched me
    and you know me.
You know when I set and when I rise;
    you perceive my thoughts from afar.
You discern my going out and my lying down;
    you are familiar with all my ways....
For you created my inmost being;
    you knit me together in my mother's womb.
I praise you because I am fearfully
    and wonderfully made;

your works are wonderful,

I know that full well.

My frame was not hidden from you

    when I was made in the secret place.

When I was woven together in the depths of the earth,

    your eyes saw my unformed body.

All the days ordained for me

    were written in your book

    before one of them came to be. (Psalm 139)

My makeup and gift mix are an extremely significant indicator of my calling. I was designed from the very beginning by God to accomplish His purpose. Based on David's psalm, would it make any sense for God to form and equip me with such precise intention, and then call me to do something that does not fit who I am? Just like our fingerprints uniquely identify us, God receives the greatest glory when our gifts find their full expression. He is not glorified when we try to be someone we were never intended to be or created to be. We might articulate that rich truth in the following way:

If God created me to serve His purpose, and if God formed and "wired" me with awesomely precise intention, then my calling should be closely aligned with my makeup.

We might have questions that revolve around the exact nature of our calling. But we should never wonder if God has made us up internally to accomplish our calling. I have been created with the exact gift mix to do what God wants me to do.

CHAPTER TWO

Four Categories for How Calling Happens

How does God call me? We researched the answer to that question by going directly to the pages of Scripture. In the Old and New Testaments there are scores of examples of men called by God into specific work situations. God's methods of calling fit into four categories:

Category 1: God calls me directly by name.

Category 2: God places a desire on my heart.

Category 3: God arranges my path.

Category 4: God prepares an attractive option.

Category 1: God calls me directly by name.

ABRAHAM

Genesis 12 begins rather abruptly: "The Lord had said to Abram, 'Leave your country, your people and your father's household and go to the land I will show you'" (Genesis 12:1).

OK! What can Abram (his name until God changed it to Abraham) say? God's call on his life was so clear, so precise, so unambiguous that there really was only one possible response.

> So Abram left, as the Lord had told him....Abram was seventy-five years old when he set out from Haran. He took his wife Sarai, his nephew Lot, all the possessions they had accumulated and the people they had acquired in Haran, and they set out for the land of Canaan, and they arrived there. (Genesis 12:4-5)

Who else experienced God's call in a similar way?

MOSES

Moses was called by name:

> Now Moses was tending the flock of Jethro his father-in-law...and he led the flock to the far side of the

desert and came to Horeb, the mountain of God. There the angel of the Lord appeared to him in flames of fire from within a bush. Moses saw that though the bush was on fire it did not burn up. So Moses thought, "I will go over and see this strange sight—why the bush does not burn up."

When the Lord saw that he had gone over to look, God called to him from within the bush, "Moses, Moses!"

And Moses said, "Here I am."

.... The Lord said, "... So now, go. I am sending you to Pharaoh to bring my people the Israelites out of Egypt." (Exodus 3:1-10)

Moses did not appreciate God's call very much, "O Lord, please send someone else to do it," but he was not left in much doubt as to what God's call was.

PAUL

Paul's call was also very dramatic. He was on his way to Damascus to persecute and imprison any Christians he found there, when Jesus confronted Paul with a light bright enough to blind him. Simultaneous with the light Paul heard the words:

"Saul, Saul, why do you persecute me?"

"Who are you, Lord?" Saul asked.

"I am Jesus, whom you are persecuting," he replied.

"Now get up and go into the city, and you will be told what you must do." (Acts 9:4-6)

Over the next few days God used a man by the name of Ananias to communicate His specific calling to Paul. The encounter changed Paul's life. Not only did he end up with a new relationship with the God of the universe, he also had a new calling and career.

God's call to Abraham, to Moses, and to Paul could not have been more direct. God addressed them directly by name and told them what their work was going to look like. In the same category are Old Testament men like Joshua, Aaron, Ezekiel, Samson, and Elijah. The New Testament list includes Matthew, Peter, James, and John the Baptist.

Sometimes God addresses me directly and calls me by name.

Category 2: God places a desire on my heart.

NEHEMIAH

Nehemiah was a troubled man. Close to the apex of power in Babylon, he had access to information. And what he heard one day caused him to sit down and weep. The walls around Jerusalem were lying in rubble, and the gates had been burned to the ground.

Nehemiah's response was dramatic: "When I heard these things, I sat down and wept. For some days I mourned and fasted and prayed before the God of heaven" (Nehemiah 1:4). He was devastated. The walls were down around the "city on a hill" that symbolized God's chosen nation. How could the Jews return from exile in Babylon to a city that lay vulnerable, unprotected, and in disgrace?

Why did the news about Jerusalem affect Nehemiah with such force? Was he so ignorant about suffering and injustice in the world that a bad report left him stunned? Of course not. He was the cupbearer to King Artaxerxes of Babylon, which was the dominant empire of the day. In today's world, Nehemiah's position would be similar to the White House chief of staff. Nehemiah heard bad news, shocking information, extremely unsettling data every hour of every working day. It goes with the territory of such a position.

But this news was different. It affected him uniquely because God wanted it to. God had it in His plan to use Nehemiah to lead the effort to rebuild the wall. The Babylonian exile was ending, and God's people were returning to the Promised Land. Nehemiah was a crucial component of God's plan to bring His people home. The burden placed on Nehemiah's heart was God's unavoidable call to a very specific task.

ISAIAH

Nehemiah heard terrible news, but Isaiah had a wonderful vision. He saw the Lord seated on a throne in the highest heaven. Above the throne were magnificent angels, each with six wings. As the angels flew they sang perpetually, "Holy, holy, holy is the Lord Almighty; the whole earth is full of his glory" (Isaiah 6:3).

There was smoke, and everything shook. Isaiah was so taken with the purity of God that his own unrighteousness overwhelmed him. He was a broken man: "'Woe to me!'" I cried. 'I am ruined! For I am a man of unclean lips, and I live among a people of unclean lips, and my eyes have seen the King, the Lord Almighty'" (Isaiah 6:5).

Then something remarkable happened. One of the angels took a live coal, touched Isaiah's mouth, and declared Isaiah's guilt gone and his sin atoned for. In an interchange that followed, God asked who would represent him, and Isaiah volunteered: "'Here am I. Send me!'" (Isaiah 6:8).

So launched the career of one of the major prophets of the Old Testament era. God called Isaiah to be His spokesman to the nation of Israel during a very turbulent time.

Sometimes I feel a responsibility to accomplish a task and meet a need (or, God places a burden on my heart).

Category 3: God arranges my path.

DANIEL

The British Museum in London has a stone panel from the palace of King Nebuchadnezzar, which depicts captives being led in chains from Jerusalem to Babylon. I have stood in front of that amazing pictorial many times, and in every instance I have thought about Daniel. Daniel was called to his career in disgrace. He was one of the captives taken from his home in the Promised Land to the capital of a powerful and pagan empire.

Daniel was called to serve and rose to be a top administrator during almost the entire captivity of the Israelites in Babylon. He did so with utmost integrity, and often at risk to his own life. In one of the most spectacular conversions of all time, Nebuchadnezzar, who was one of the cruelest rulers of his day, became a follower of God though Daniel's influence: "Now I, Nebuchadnezzar, praise and exalt and glorify the King of heaven, because everything he does is right and all his ways are just. And those who walk in pride he is able to humble" (Daniel 4:37).

Daniel served four kings in three empires. He was so valuable that even when the empire changed hands, from the Babylonians to the Medes to the Persians, Daniel stayed in place. He was very good at what he did. He was called to his career. As a captive, he had no choice.

JOSIAH

When Josiah came out of the womb, his life career had already been decided; he just didn't know it yet. But he found out quickly. He was eight years old when he became king of

Judah, and he ruled in Jerusalem for thirty-one years (2 Kings 22).

Josiah was a direct descendant of David, the great king of Israel. During David's reign God promised him that his house, or family, would rule forever. So as with the House of Windsor in Great Britain, whose clearly established line of succession determines who rules next, Josiah was born into royal obligation.

Josiah was called to be king. His calling and career did not involve any choice on his part. There were no list of options from what to choose. His calling was decided for him.

Sometimes a job simply shows up at my door (or, God arranges my career track without my input).

Category 4: God prepares an attractive option.

ELISHA

Elisha's calling was almost cryptic, but then I guess that is what you would expect if you were recruited by a prophet. Elisha was working on the farm. More specifically, he was plowing with twelve yoke of oxen. All of the sudden Elijah the prophet came up to him and threw his cloak around him.

Elisha then left his oxen and ran after Elijah. "Let me kiss my father and mother good-by," he said, "and then I will come with you." "Go back," Elijah replied. "What have I done to you?" So Elisha left him and went back. He took his yoke of oxen and slaughtered them. He burned the plowing equipment to cook the meat and gave it to the people, and they ate. Then he set out to follow Elijah and became his attendant. (1 Kings 19:20-21)

Elisha had an extraordinary career. He was mentored by Elijah, until Elijah was suddenly taken up to heaven in a whirlwind of chariots and horses of fire. Then Elisha was on his own. Somehow he felt called to choose a relationship and a career with Elijah. Which was exactly what God had created him to do.

STEPHEN

We remember Stephen primarily because he was stoned to death for his faith. He was the first Christian martyr, following Christ's ascension into heaven. But he first comes to our attention in Acts 6.

The young church in Jerusalem was straining under the weight of its exponential growth. The apostles, who were called to lead the church, found themselves consumed with a myriad of operational details. They decided that a different organizational structure was needed.

> So the Twelve gathered all the disciples together and said, "It would not be right for us to neglect the ministry of the word of God in order to wait on tables [the operational problem of the moment]. Brothers, choose seven men from among you who are known to be full of the Spirit and wisdom. We will turn this responsibility over to them and will give our attention to prayer and the ministry of the word." (Acts 6:2-4)

Stephen was one of those chosen. It might have looked to be a simple case of being in the right place at the right time. He just happened to be available. But Stephen's calling was far more than simple coincidence. God, in his sovereignty, had prepared Stephen and placed him exactly where he could be "chosen." What looked like a serendipitous employment opportunity was really God's way of calling a man.

Sometimes I respond to an employment opportunity (or, I am led to "choose" a work option that God prepared and made attractive).

God uses different ways to call me regarding my work. Apart from a direct word from God, the work I am called to often looks and feels like the coincidental intersection between a job opportunity, my makeup, and leading from the Holy Spirit. The next chapter paints a picture of three current-day examples of what calling looks like.

CHAPTER THREE

What Calling Looks Like

C alling of men does not only happen in the pages of Scripture. As is clear from what we have learned in this book, all of us are called.

Larry Wheeler (not his real name), Milton Lentz, and Rich Brown are all friends of ours. They are "called" men, but to different careers. Larry is a top executive in a Fortune 50 company. Milton owns his own construction company. Rich is a physician and surgeon. What follows is a description of each of their callings.

The executive: Larry Wheeler

Larry Wheeler heard a calling when he graduated from college, but it wasn't from the Lord.

As one of the top graduates from Ohio University in 1970, Larry was getting calls from all quarters—including Harvard

Business School. The one he decided to answer, though, was from a large multinational corporation.

Larry had seen enough of the classroom. He was ready for the boardroom. He was ready to make his move onto the corporate fast track, where he just knew he would lap the field.

And he did, too. But in rising to a position as a vice president of a Fortune 50 company, Larry discovered that another plan, one larger and much more dynamic than his own, also was in the works. And as he rose up each rung of the corporate ladder, he not only achieved secular success but placed himself in a position for spiritual success as well.

Larry was living in the town of his company's corporate offices when he discovered Christ. But it wasn't until he moved to another location and launched an innovative customer business development division that he gained a real sense of his calling and how it fit into his professional life.

In helping engineer a partnership relationship with his company's largest customer, Larry began to explore the idea of linking business principles with biblical wisdom. Every time a decision had to be made in this highly stressful, ultracompetitive secular business setting, he turned to the Bible for practical solutions. And every time he turned to look for answers, God provided them.

Despite resistance from top executives at both companies, God continued to affirm and reaffirm Larry's approach with answers to problems and positive bottom-line results that silenced the critics.

The model Larry helped develop now is used worldwide by his company, even though many of those who are using it are unaware that the ideas behind it came not from a business book but from the greatest best-seller of all time—the Bible.

Larry is a mentor and a leader to other men all over the world, not just for his extraordinary talents as an executive, but also for his steady display of godly character.

But Larry has been able to model on more than just a personal level. While that is an important part of his calling in the workplace, it is only one part. Another is the actual model he helped create for his company—a model founded and constructed with biblical principles and yet a model that significantly outperforms systems designed by man.

The examples of his life and the business system he helped create serve as testimonies for numerous men and women at numerous different levels within the secular world. They allow others to see how the power and wisdom of God can work outside of what traditionally are considered "religious" settings.

The builder: Milton Lentz

The foundations for the eight thousand-square-foot house are dug into a hilltop that overlooks other hilltops and valleys and all of the other wonders of this particular edge of the Ozark Mountains.

When it is completed, the owner will have a majestic view, one befitting his status as a well-to-do member of an area filled with well-to-do members. He will be able to pull his expensive car through his expensive gate and drive up his expensive drive to an expensive house filled with expensive furnishings.

But he will rest easily in the knowledge that this project was a bargain. For one thing, he knows the man building it for him would never cheat him by padding his bills or cutting corners. It just wouldn't happen. And when he opens his eyes and his heart, he finds an even-more-valuable fringe benefit from the construction firm he hired—the quiet example of the man who owns it.

Milton Lentz wasn't just called to work in the construction business, he was born into it.

When he was three years old and his father headed off to a construction site, Milton went right along with him, just as his father had done at the hands of Milton's grandfather.

If his father had been a mechanic, Milton might well be a mechanic today. But his father worked in construction. And for most of his forty-two years on this earth, so has Milton.

However, Milton learned early on that he wasn't being forced into a vocation simply to maintain the family tradition. He discovered he had real talents that merely were being developed by his environment. Milton can hammer a two-inch nail into a four-inch-wide board directly above his head faster than most men can pull that same nail from the pouch in their work belt.

Milton tested the waters once. As a young adult he went to work at a carpet store. It didn't take long for Milton to realize he wasn't a salesman. For one thing, he was too color-blind to tell customers honestly if this carpet matched that wallpaper. For another, he simply wasn't cut out to push products on a daily basis.

Luckily, Milton's house burned. It didn't seem so lucky at the time, of course. But that misfortune provided an insurance check that allowed Milton to escape what fast was becoming a suffocating job and the debt that was coming with it.

So Milton returned to a more natural calling, one that God had confirmed to him many times before and would confirm to him many times after.

Milton sees that confirmation in the projects he voluntarily built at several locations across the country for the Torchbearers of the Capernwray Missionary Fellowship which operates Bible schools and summer camps.

He sees that confirmation in each new client, especially those who show up unexpectedly when they are needed the most. He couldn't make a living selling carpet, he will point out, but God continues to provide homes and offices for him to build.

And he sees that confirmation in people like the man who wants the big house up on the hill. Milton never brings up God when he is working on that job. He never forces his testimony on the man who is paying the bills. But the man simply can't resist asking, because he can't help seeing God work through the life of his contractor.

The surgeon: Rich Brown

It wasn't until Rich Brown gave up on his dream to become an eye surgeon that God helped it come true.

After four years of college and four years of medical school, Rich was ready to begin his residency in ophthalmology (if you can spell it, he says, you're board certified). He was fascinated by the eye and vividly recalled the two surgeries he needed as a child to straighten the muscles surrounding his eyes. This, it seemed, was his calling.

Rich always had a general sense of what God wanted him to do with his professional life. But the older he has become, the more specific that call has become.

He grew up in a Christian home. The fact that God had a plan for him was taught at an early age, and he never really considered that he might do something that wasn't in line with God's purpose.

By the time he was ready to graduate from elementary school, Rich already felt a calling for service. And by dreaming and praying about what that meant, he soon was led into medicine. His family had a history of attending college, but he would be the first doctor.

He spent a year at West Point learning that he did not want to become a military doctor. But he still knew he wanted to practice medicine. It wasn't until he was in medical school that he began to think about the eye surgeries he had undergone as a child. While walking home from class each day, he began to think about a career in vision.

But when it came time to find a residency, Rich faced one rather large problem: He had nowhere to go.

Like all would-be doctors, Rich had submitted his list of preferred residency choices. The residency programs submitted their lists of preferred doctors. When the two lists came together, there was no match for Rich in ophthalmology.

Naturally, he was devastated—so devastated, in fact, that he ended up in a mental hospital. Not as a patient, although he admits that maybe he should have been. Rich was working part-time as a night admissions officer at a mental-health facility in Little Rock. The workload was light, so Rich turned his attention to prayer. Despite his desire to become an eye surgeon, he gave his career over to God. He would do, he said, whatever God instructed, even if it meant a residency in his least favorite of fields—ob-gyn.

Suddenly, a peace came over Rich Brown. For the first time since he learned the news about his residency, he was able to rest.

The next morning, two hours into a shift at Arkansas Children's Hospital, Rich got a call from his father. It seems a doctor at the University of Missouri-Kansas City had been unable to reach Rich through other channels, and he needed to talk to the young physician. UMKC had an unexpected opening the doctor thought Rich could fill—a residency in ophthalmology.

Rich, now thirty-nine with ten years of experience as an ophthalmologist, has seen that calling confirmed in many ways. He has seen it in the people he works with—patients, doctors, and staff. He has seen it in the amount of time being in his profession gives him to devote to other ministries. And he saw it three years ago when he was having a crisis in confidence while trying to adjust to new surgical techniques. His colleagues rallied to support him and reaffirmed his natural talent for surgery.

But his most recent confirmation that he is serving where God wants him came when he and his family were selected for a work-mission trip in Gilgit, Pakistan, for the 1997 summer.

When Rich e-mailed the dates he would be available, he got a quick and enthusiastic reply. The dates corresponded with the dates when one of the two doctors at the clinic would be in London for a training course. He would be coming at the time the clinic needed him most—there to help man and serve God as an ophthalmologist, just as he had originally dreamed.

Conclusion

C alling is God's personal invitation for each Christian to work on His agenda, utilizing our created talents to do something that is eternally significant.

Finding and living out our calling are absolutely essential steps in the making of a godly man. If we know our calling, then we can serve God's purpose and enjoy meaning and satisfaction.

On our Buffalo River fishing trip a couple of years ago, we had to navigate around some very rough water before we could delight in the heaven-on-earth exhilaration that every true fisherman knows.

Calling is very much the same. The earlier in our work life that we discover our calling, the longer we will have to revel in our job fit and delight in our career niche.

Calling happens. Why? Because God loves us enough to create us with precision and use us for something eternally significant.

Thank you, Lord.

"When David had served God's purpose in his own generation, he fell asleep" (Acts 13:36).

Where Do I Go from Here?

1. *Come to God in brokenness, with an intense passion to understand His Word and hear His voice.*

   We will only know our calling if He tells us. He is the key to our calling. Finding our calling is a spiritual exercise in which I turn my face toward God in both Bible study and prayer, with specific intent to know His will regarding my vocation.

2. *Pray, think, and talk your way through chapter 2, "Four Categories for How Calling Happens."*

   As you look back on your pilgrimage through life and as you evaluate your present situation, what clues do you have to help explain your calling? What do people who know you well say about your calling when they look at you through the lens of the four categories?

3. *Distinguish between the kind of work you do and the actual job you have.*

If you are unhappy in your current situation, determine whether your dissatisfaction comes from the kind of work your job requires, or from your work environment, or from both. Our best reading of Scripture leaves us convinced that God calls us to do the kind of work we are suited for. However, He may call us to do the kind of work that we are suited for in an environment that is very imperfect. Figuring out what action to take depends on knowing the reasons for your unhappiness.

4. *Be patient.*

God makes His will clear to us in His time. We cannot rush what He is not doing quickly. View this as a process over time, not an event in time.

Notes for Personal Reflection

Chapter One

_____

_____

_____

_____

_____

_____

_____

_____

_____

_____

_____

_____

_____

_____

Chapter Two

Chapter Three

_____

_____

_____

_____

_____

_____

_____

_____

_____

_____

_____

_____

_____

_____

_____

_____

If you liked this book and would like to know more about ™Life@Work Cͦ™ or Cornerstone please call us at 1-800-739-7863.

Other ways to reach us:

Mail: Post Office Box 1928
         Fayetteville, AR 72702

Fax: (501) 443-4125

E-mail: LifeWork@CornerstoneCo.com